A short history

In AD 7... ...astal
lowlan... ...eir
aim to ... ...ere
their ne... ...ey
built a f... ...heir
general, ...e fort
of Didius. A thousand years later, the Normans,
following a similar agenda, built a fort on the same
site. Its 12th-century stone replacement now stands
in the grounds of Cardiff Castle.

For centuries, Cardiff remained a small market town,
huddled around the castle. However, its importance
as a port was growing, which unfortunately made
it a magnet for the 'rioters, cut-throats and pirates
who infested the Bristol Channel'. This reputation
brought decline – by the 18th century only 1,500
people were living here.

However, things were stirring in the valleys to the
north. In 1550, iron ore was found. Coal, too, was
discovered. Furnaces sprang up everywhere. In
1794, the Glamorganshire Canal linked Merthyr
Tydfil's massive ironworks with Cardiff's beckoning
bay. At last, iron could be exported in the quantity
demanded by the Industrial Revolution. Enter the
2nd Marquess of Bute (1793–1848), who owned
large estates in Wales. In 1839 he put the entire
family fortune into building Bute West Dock, linked
to the valleys by railway. Soon, exports of coal
outstripped those of iron. Within a few years sleepy
Cardiff became a sprawling industrial port, its five
vast docks the destination of the tramp steamers and
colliers of the world. 'Tiger Bay' also became home
to an amazing mix of races, religions and languages.
The trade brought the 3rd Marquess of Bute
(1847–1900) great wealth. A reluctant businessman,
he ploughed much of it into his homes, notably
Cardiff Castle and Castell Coch, and into patronage
reflecting his diverse interests. His legacy remains in
many of Cardiff's beautiful buildings and parks.

The coal trade peaked in 1913 and has now virtually
gone. A city from 1905, Cardiff became Wales's
capital 50 years later. Since then, the once grim port
has reinvented itself yet again, largely through its
stunningly redeveloped docklands.

View across Cardiff Bay

Cardiff Castle

There has been a castle here for 2,000 years, since Roman times. The impressive keep, which the Normans built nearly 900 years ago, still stands. However, what makes Cardiff Castle particularly special is the amazing interior of the house within its walls, sumptuously decorated for the 3rd Marquess of Bute by Gothic-revival architect William Burges (see pages 4–5).

The Norman keep

To consolidate their invasion of 1066, the Normans hurriedly threw up motte-and-bailey castles. These comprised a mound (motte), overlooking an enclosed courtyard (the bailey), with a wooden keep on the top. In time, these motte-and-bailey castles were replaced by those made of stone. Cardiff's keep dates from around 1140, reinforced by an outer south tower at the turn of the 14th century. In landscaping the grounds, designer Lancelot 'Capability' Brown demolished these outer works in 1777.

The Roman wall

In 1889, excavations on behalf of the 3rd Marquess of Bute revealed Roman foundations of 3 metres (10 feet) thick. These were the remains of the walls that surrounded the fourth Roman fortress, built in the late 3rd or early 4th century and corresponding to the square site we see today. True to form, the Marquess resolved to have them rebuilt, a process that took his masons 35 years.

The keep

A chequered history

In the early 15th century, Richard Beauchamp, Earl of Warwick, built a new tower and hall where the house now stands. Later, the Herberts, Earls of Pembroke, made the building a luxurious house, but the English Civil War saw it fall into disrepair. However, when a Herbert descendant married Lord Mountstuart in 1766, the future 1st Marquess of Bute remodelled the house and transformed the grounds. The work was finished by the 2nd Marquess, the man who created the docks and, thus, the family fortune. Then came the 3rd Marquess. As the opulence of the house shows, he was more interested in spending money than making it.

The castle residence

Firing Line Museum

This museum, housed in the Interpretation Centre at Cardiff Castle, is packed with over 300 years of the history relating to two regiments who have played a significant role in many of Britain's major conflicts: the 1st The Queen's Dragoon Guards and The Royal Welsh. The museum provides a greater understanding of the history of the Welsh soldier, with stories and memories from those who have dedicated their lives to the armed services.

Cardiff Castle

Bute and Burges

The 3rd Marquess of Bute, a respected amateur historian and one of Europe's wealthiest men, was famous for his love of building and restoration. Declaring that the castle 'was far from setting an example in art', he asked Gothic-revival architect William Burges (1827–81) to remodel it. For Burges, the 'art architect', this was a dream commission. He and Bute shared several passions: for the Middle Ages, for foreign travel, for spirituality (in its broadest sense), for humour. These themes were liberally poured into his designs. As if with the slow sweep of a wand, he transformed what had been a worthy but dull castle into a sumptuous fantasyland.

Clock Tower

Towering masterpiece

Bute wanted towers; he got them. Burges created several: the Clock, the Guest, the Tank Towers, and heightened others: the Herbert, Octagon and Bute Towers. Beneath this dramatic skyline he conjured up equally exotic and amazing interiors.

Winter Smoking Room

Winter Smoking Room

This room, where Victorian gentlemen retired to smoke their cigars, caused a sensation on its completion in 1872. On a tour of the castle, it is overpowering in its ornateness, a riot of green, gold, stained glass, inlaid wood and a wonderful chimneypiece frieze. The room is located within the Clock Tower and symbols of the passing of time are everywhere: the seasons, the days of the week, the signs of the zodiac.

Arab Room ceiling

Children's Day Nursery

Arab Room

Burges's last room in the castle is his most exotic. In this chamber, designed as an occasional sitting room, comfort comes second to marble and gilt, ostentatious but fantastic to behold. The crowning glory is the stalactite ceiling, tapering upwards in sculpted mini-alcoves to an Arabic rose design at the central point. It is gilded with 22-carat Welsh gold and embellished with animals and birds, in particular the parrots that Burges was so fond of. Its remarkable effect is best seen by looking directly up from the centre of the room.

Children's Day Nursery

The nursery was where the Butes' four children spent most of their formative years. Around the walls are tiled friezes of famous myths and fairy tales: Ali Baba, Puss in Boots, George and the Dragon, and more. These, together with the many toys on display, represent the carefree aspects of childhood, while a typically Victorian cautionary note, illustrating the dangers that fame and wealth may bring, lurks in the carved chimneypiece.

Banqueting Hall

Lord Bute wanted a centrepiece to his new 'medieval' castle, and Burges demolished seven bedrooms to achieve it. The project began in 1872, but was only finished in 1890, long after Burges's death. It has since fulfilled its function of entertainment on a grand scale, and several generations of royalty have dined here. Around the sides, murals and stained glass tell the history of the castle, while heraldic shields within the magnificent roof reflect the 3rd Marquess's Scottish ancestry.

Banqueting Hall

City Centre

Cardiff is noted for its delightful Victorian and Edwardian shopping arcades, airy passages with glass roofs and galleries, populated by a great variety of shops, cafés and – above them – offices. These tend to follow the lines of the old alleys and lanes of the medieval town. Each arcade has its own character, but amongst the most notable are the well-preserved Morgan Arcade (1896) with its original wood-framed shop fronts and Venetian windows on the first floor, and the L-shaped Castle Arcade (1887), which has three storeys at one end and a cast-iron bridge linking its balconies.

The Cardiff Story

This interactive museum is housed in the charming Old Library building in the heart of the city and tells the tale of the transformation of Cardiff from its humble beginnings as a small market town to the exciting capital city it has become.

The Cardiff in Context gallery is very much a hands-on experience – fascinating for all ages. It consists of three areas: A Port of Some Importance enables visitors to discover why people first settled in Cardiff; Changing Cardiff shows how the success of the docks in the 19th century impacted on the development of the city and how residents were affected; Working Lives explores how local people have made their living from the land, the sea and industry. City Lab is another interactive learning gallery, where families can explore Cardiff's history through activities, displays and a research library. There are changing exhibitions in the first-floor galleries too.

The Cardiff Story

Morgan Arcade in the Morgan Quarter   *St David's Dewi Sant shopping centre and the Central Library*

The Old Library

In 1862 Cardiff was the first town in Wales to adopt the Public Libraries Act of 1855, whereby a penny rate was levied by the council to provide a free library. The Old Library building, now housing The Cardiff Story, opened in 1882, its construction funded by the penny rate. It not only provided the people of Cardiff with a free library, but also a museum and schools for science and art. The building was extended in the 1890s, again funded by the penny rate, and continued to be the city's library until 1988.

The splendid Victorian design includes a tiled corridor with wall tiles depicting the four seasons, morning and night. The floor tiles appear to be mosaic, though it is in fact the use of coloured clay in their design that gives this impression. Although the heating system is modern, sympathetic renovations have retained some of the original – and particularly rare – vertical-style heaters which were installed by John Williams & Sons of Cardiff.

St David's Dewi Sant

A short walk from the railway and bus stations, in the heart of the city, this retail and leisure complex is one of Europe's leading 21st-century tourist destinations offering everything a modern-day shopper could desire.

With the soaring Grand Arcade as its centrepiece, and with Welsh stone, timber and other natural materials used in its construction, a sense of space is created in the midst of famous stores that go hand-in-hand with public art, a variety of restaurants and residential apartments.

Central Library

The award-winning Central Library for Cardiff opened in March 2009. This iconic library building was created as part of the St David's Dewi Sant complex. The energy-efficient building provides educational materials, information and entertainment over six storeys.

The artwork at the entrance is by Jean Bernard Metais, while wall art inside features the work of Neil Canning, illustrating light and weather on the landscape and sea.

As well as traditional books the library has interactive materials, along with quiet study space. Music is an added feature here, with specially designed music pods provided – and even a grand piano, which the public can book to play.

City Centre

St John's Church

Cardiff's parish church dates mainly from the 15th century, the original Norman church being destroyed during the Welsh nationalist leader Owain Glyndwr's rebellion against the English (1400–15). The nave was rebuilt in the Perpendicular style, the work being completed in 1473 by the soaring tower, which, for centuries, dominated the town. Amongst many fine features within are the carved heads in the chancel, several ancient memorials, two gilded reredoses, and stained glass by, amongst others, William Morris, Edward Burne-Jones, Sir Ninian Comper and Ford Madox Brown.

St John's Church

Queen Street statues

Around the city centre, and especially on pedestrianized Queen Street, are many bronze figures by Welsh sculptor Robert Thomas (1926–99). These include *Mother and Son* (1963), *Miner* (1993) and, most famously, a 1987 statue of Aneurin ('Nye') Bevan (1897–1960). Bevan was a Welsh politician who, in 1948, as Secretary of State for Health, pioneered the formation of the National Health Service, overcoming considerable opposition in achieving this.

'Miner', by Robert Thomas

Beautiful ballast

The former Ebeneser Chapel in Charles Street is unique. The ships that took Welsh coal to the rest of the world returned laden with ballast – all manner of rocks, irregular in type, shape and colour – used to keep 'empty' vessels stable. Architect R.G. Thomas used this stone to build the chapel. As well as being an excellent early example of recycling, the stones were intended to represent God's universal power.

Ebeneser Chapel wall

Cardiff Central Market

Cardiff's covered market has an impressive number of stalls (around 70) selling a huge variety of items, from fresh food to jewellery to pots and pans. The cast-iron and glass building seen today was opened in 1891, distinguished for its galleried sides and the decorative clock over the central office. In the 18th century, the market was almost the only place in Cardiff to buy life's necessities. Today's market, as well as being a must for visitors, is still very much a focal point where locals go for fine local produce and personal, friendly service.

Cardiff Central Market

Sport for all

Although Cardiff is world renowned for its link with rugby, it also has many other sporting facilities in and around the city, not least of all its well-supported football team: Cardiff City FC ('The Bluebirds'). After 99 years at Ninian Park, the club moved to its new home ground at Cardiff City Stadium in 2009; Cardiff's rugby union team ('Cardiff Blues') also plays here. Another superb site is Cardiff International Sports Stadium, an athletics, multi-sport and special events venue. The city is also home to the SWALEC Stadium, set in beautiful parkland and home to Glamorgan Cricket Club. The stadium was proud to host its first Ashes Test Match in 2009.

St David's RC Cathedral

St David's, on Charles Street, was a Pugin Company church that was elevated to cathedral status in 1916. It was built in 1887 as a response to the huge influx of Irish Roman Catholics who came over to work on the construction of the docks and railways. Bombed during the Second World War, the church was restored in the 1950s.

Roath Park

Roath Park

Although situated to the north-east of the city, this park with its huge lake is probably the most popular public open space for Cardiff city residents. Almost inevitably, Roath Park was a gift to the people from the 3rd Marquess of Bute. Now people come here to sit or stroll round the lakeside, feed the waterbirds or take a ride in a rowing boat or pleasure cruiser.

Civic Centre

Cardiff's Civic Centre is one of the world's finest. It was created from Cathays Park, once a Bute property, in the 1890s, a time when the town hall, courts, museum and university all needed larger premises. The 3rd Marquess stipulated that only public buildings should be built here, and that the avenue of elm trees (later destroyed by disease) should remain. These provisos dictated its shape.

City Hall clock tower

City Hall

Begun as a town hall in 1901, this handsome neoclassical building was opened as City Hall in 1906. For years, shire horses pulled huge blocks of Portland (Dorset) stone up from the docks to be cut and carved on site. City Hall's principal features are the 59-metre (194-foot) clock tower and the central dome, beneath which is the Council Chamber. The superb Marble Hall features several fine statues of Welsh heroes.

Friary Gardens

These small gardens are notable not only for their neat topiary but also for the statue of the 3rd Marquess of Bute, who had such an influence on Cardiff's development, status and wealth.

Civic Centre Buildings

Several fine public buildings grace Cathays Park. Like City Hall, the oldest ones are classical in style and faced with Portland stone. Of the trio of buildings at the front, the 1904 Law Courts (left of City Hall) present the sternest face to the city; the National Museum of Wales building (right of City Hall; see more details on pages 12–13) dates from 1927. To the north of the park, several classical-style buildings now belong to universities.

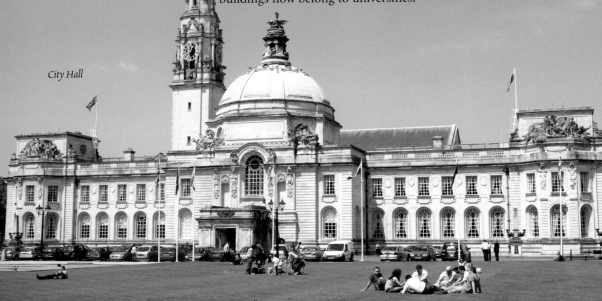

City Hall

The dock feeder

An insignificant-looking waterway creeps along in a cutting on the south side of the Boulevard de Nantes near the New Theatre, where it disappears into a culvert. This is the dock feeder, which was once important to Cardiff's economy. Built in 1834, it brought water from the Glamorganshire Canal into the first Bute dock, to help scour away the mud that the tides brought in.

3rd Marquess of Bute statue, Friary Gardens

Alexandra Gardens

Alexandra Gardens is the green heart of Cathays Park. At its centre, the Welsh National War Memorial (1928), designed by Sir Ninian Comper, commemorates soldiers, sailors and airmen of Wales who lost their lives in the First World War. Bronzes symbolizing these heroes raise wreaths towards the winged messenger of Victory. A plaque was added in memory of men and women who died in the Second World War. Elsewhere are other memorials to men of Cardiff killed in the 1982 Falklands War and to all those who fought in the International Brigade during the Spanish Civil War of 1936–9.

Gorsedd Gardens

Thousands of students and workers pass through these gardens, with their lovely floral displays, en route to and from the Civic Centre buildings. The Gorsedd is the assembly of Bards responsible for the Welsh cultural festival known as the National Eisteddfod. The stone circle in Gorsedd Gardens is not as ancient as it may look; it was built of sandstone (from Penarth across the bay) for the National Eisteddfod of 1899 and moved here from the nearby Eisteddfod site in 1905.

The 1960 bronze statue of David Lloyd George (1863–1945) by Michael Rizzello stands opposite the National Museum Cardiff. Lloyd George was MP for Caernarfon for 55 years, a famous Liberal Chancellor and Prime Minister (1916–22).

Welsh National War Memorial, Alexandra Gardens

National Museum Cardiff

The National Museum is proud to be popular with visitors of all ages and interests. It is home to spectacular collections from Wales and all over the world. Unusually, it has art, archaeology, geology and natural history all under one roof. Particularly special is the Evolution of Wales, which takes you on an exciting journey from the Big Bang to the present day, while the art collection, especially the array of Impressionist paintings, is of great beauty and international importance.

Evolution of Wales

In this gallery, a dramatic 4,600 million-year journey through the geological periods shows how the landscape of Wales evolved before humans came on the scene. First, we see the powerful influence of earthquakes, volcanoes and movements in the Earth's crust. In particular, we find out about the rocks, such as coal, which have become important to Wales. Impressive skeletons and life-size models bring to life the era when dinosaurs and woolly mammoths roamed a Wales covered by tropical forest.

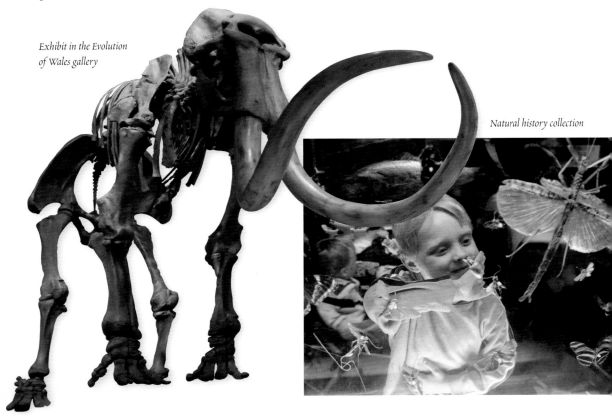

Exhibit in the Evolution of Wales gallery

Natural history collection

National Museum Cardiff

Artes Mundi

Award-winning Artes Mundi (Latin for 'Arts of the World') is a major international visual art event that takes place at the National Museum of Cardiff every two years. Established in 2003, this contemporary visual arts initiative celebrates artists from all around the world, with particular emphasis on social and political themes. As well as a magnificent exhibition being staged, a significant prize is awarded to one artist each time the event is held.

Origins: in Search of Early Wales

This exciting gallery brings to life the background of the men and women who helped create the Wales of today, revealing what life was like for people from the Stone Age to the end of the Middle Ages. The gallery highlights recent archaeological discoveries and sheds new light on old treasures. Among the top features are: a cast of the Red Lady of Paviland, the UK's earliest human remains, 250,000 years old; the Iron-Age Capel Garmon firedog; a Roman leopard cup from Abergavenny; and a superb Viking sword rescued from the depths off the coast of Pembrokeshire.

National Museum of Art

Within the National Museum Cardiff is the National Museum of Art, one of Britain's finest collections, that tells the story of Welsh art. The exhibits include fine Impressionist and Post-Impressionist artworks. The collection owes its existence to the generosity of two wealthy sisters, Gwendoline (died 1951) and Margaret Davies (died 1963). Avid art collectors from the early years of the 20th century, they bequeathed to the museum all 260 of the works they acquired. Amongst the many delights in the collection are Renoir's *La Parisienne*, a version of Rodin's *The Kiss*, several paintings by Monet and others by Cezanne, Van Gogh, Manet, Pissarro, Millet, Daumier and Carrière.

Renoir's 'La Parisienne'

Rodin's 'The Kiss'

Along the Taff

It's a strong possibility that 'Taffy', the nickname for the archetypal Welshman, comes from the fine river that flows from its twin sources in the Brecon Beacons, past Merthyr Tydfil down to Cardiff Bay. Its peaceful banks provide lovely walks within and beyond the city.

Bute Park and the River Taff

Taff Trail

Launched in 1988 for walkers and cyclists, the trail follows the river upstream from Cardiff through the Valleys to Brecon. Technically, it begins at the Roald Dahl Plass (see page 19), going via James Street to join the river on the far side of Clarence Bridge. A more scenic start takes you to the Taff via Techniquest (see page 19), the Wetlands, the sailing club, and Hamadryad Park beneath and beyond the A4232 flyover. The simplest way of all is to head for the Millennium Walkway to join the riverside path in Bute Park.

Bute Park

This lovely park by the banks of the Taff was designed in the late 19th century and given to the city, with the castle, by the 5th Marquess of Bute in 1947. Now citizens and visitors enjoy a 'green lung' close to the city centre.

The park's huge size (138 acres/56 hectares) and variety of habitats make it a haven for wildlife, and there are also various historical sites, including the ruins of a Dominican friary. Whatever the season, the park's principal delight, however, is its collection of trees: rare and ornamental ones in the arboretum; more common – but no less beautiful – species scattered throughout the park. As part of a 21st-century restoration programme, an Education Centre on the site of the plant nursery provides a wealth of information for visitors. There is a waterbus stop in the park, from which a trip can be taken downriver to Cardiff Bay.

The animal wall

The amazing stone animals on the street wall to the west of Cardiff Castle and on the southern edge of Bute Park were designed by William Burges in 1866, but only brought to life in 1890, nine years after his death. Originally they kept their eyes on passers-by from the front of the castle, but were moved and more animals added in 1925 when Castle Street was widened.

Millennium Stadium

Millennium Walkway

Millennium Stadium

The home of Welsh Rugby Union opened in 1999 and hosted the Rugby World Cup final that year. This 74,500-seater venue is one of the world's great arenas, and the first in Britain with a retractable roof. Supporting the weight of the roof accounts for the massive pointed cantilevers, which stretch out from the corners of the stadium in spectacular fashion.

The stadium also plays host to many other events including concerts, football matches and speedway. For even non-sports enthusiasts, tours of the stadium, available most days, are a fascinating experience. Not only do you venture behind the scenes – the dressing rooms, the hospitality boxes, the overwhelming walk out onto the pitch – but you also come away with some memorable facts.

Millennium Walkway

A stroll between castle and station along this £12.5 million boardwalk, suspended above the River Taff, is one of Cardiff's 'must-do' activities. From here, between 7 in the morning until 7 at night (except on match days), you get a chance to marvel at the mighty angular cantilevers that thrust out from the Millennium Stadium high above.

Cardiff Bay

An amazing transformation has been wrought in Cardiff Bay in recent years. The end of Cardiff's coal trade presented Wales's capital with a challenge: to restore the city's dented prestige, and an opportunity: to redevelop a vast area of derelict dockland. Building a barrage across the bay has resulted in a stunning new waterfront, heritage buildings side by side with impressive new landmark architecture and art. Anchoring the sparkling leisure and commercial area of today to Butetown (aka Tiger Bay), the grubby coalport of the past, is the Pierhead Building, which stands proudly at the gateway to the former coal docks.

Pierhead Building

This imposing brick and terracotta building, opened in 1896, was designed by William Frame (former assistant to William Burges) as the head office of the Bute Dock Company. Like Burges's work in Cardiff Castle, it has more than a touch of French Gothic about it. The clock was the work of Potts of Leeds who also made England's Big Ben. In recent years the iconic Pierhead has become an events and conference centre for the people of Wales, with a public space with exhibitions for visitors to enjoy.

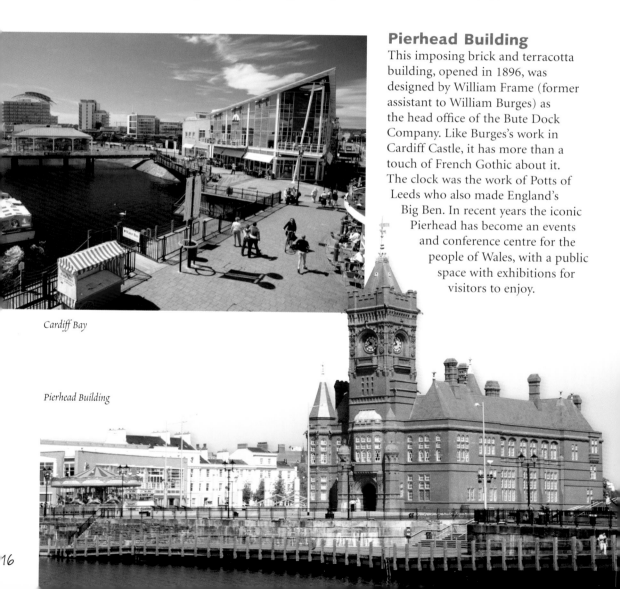

Cardiff Bay

Pierhead Building

Coal Exchange

In Mount Stuart Square, west of Bute Street, is the building that most prominently symbolized Cardiff's huge wealth and intense activity. Built 1883–6, the Coal Exchange was the place that industrialists, shipowners, merchants and speculators met to strike their deals. In this building the world's first £1 million business transaction was made. Now restored, it is a conference and entertainment venue.

Coal Exchange

Bygone Butetown

Bute Street was once the main artery of one of the world's largest industrial ports. Tiger Bay was a cosmopolitan mixture of races, religions and languages. Famously harmonious and happy, the area was home to at least 50 nationalities in the 1950s. Now, the docks have disappeared, as have the homes of the sailors and dockworkers. The Butetown History and Arts Centre on Bute Street is a 'must' to visit for anyone keen to look at the area's rich history. The centre has a huge oral and visual archive, many paintings and sculptures, plus a memorable collection of Bert Hardy Picture Post images of bygone Butetown.

Norwegian Church

Author Roald Dahl was christened in this pretty landmark, now an arts centre, gallery and cultural venue with an excellent coffee shop. The church was dismantled and moved from its original site when development at Atlantic Wharf was under way. Now reconstructed in its 1889 layout, it was in this form a church and mission serving the thousands of Scandinavians who sailed from Cardiff. Although originally of unglamorous corrugated iron, it was said to be 'the cosiest and most beautifully kept seamen's mission in Britain'.

Norwegian Church

Craft in the Bay

This superb gallery (with café) features modern craft of an exceptionally high standard. Dramatic in appearance, it is set within a reconstruction of a 19th-century dockside transit shed. Its iron frame is original, the glass cladding and thrusting roof modern and imaginative. Outside, brick paving names some of the goods that came in and out of the building in its former life.

Cardiff Bay

Wales Millennium Centre

The architects' brief for this iconic arts venue, opened in 2004, read, 'it has to be unmistakably Welsh and internationally outstanding'. Its award-winning design certainly achieves this, reflecting the country's industrial heritage and incorporating local materials – slate, steel, glass and wood. Its central space is a 1,900-seat auditorium, in sweeping laminated shapes of Welsh hardwoods. Besides major performances, a huge range of other activities go on here in the many studios, exhibition rooms, galleries and rehearsal suites within the Centre. The WMC is home to several of Wales's arts organizations. In the spectacular concourse, free daily arts performances are given, and there are several excellent restaurants, bistros and bars.

Wales Millennium Centre

The Senedd

This outward-looking, environmentally sensitive, building is the home of the National Assembly for Wales. Designed by Richard Rogers, it was officially opened in 2006. It has three floors, the heart being the circular siambr (debating chamber) beneath a dramatic timber funnel opening towards the sky. Members of the public enter at first floor level, going up to the Oriel (gallery), from where they can look down at the debates going on in the chamber, or look outwards over Cardiff Bay. In and around this fine building are many examples of art and craft, adding beauty and often functionality. Free tours of the Senedd are also available.

The Senedd

Cardiff Bay Trail

This traffic-free circular trail for walkers and cyclists runs for just over 6 miles (10km) around the Bay and over the water, via Pont Y Werin (meaning 'People's Bridge'), to Penarth. Many historic landmarks can be spotted en route, and the waterside restaurants and cafés make enjoyable stopping places. Details of the route are available from the Wales Millennium Centre.

Art in the Bay

As part of its new identity, Cardiff Bay has over 40 wonderful and varied examples of public art. For example, *A Wife on the Ocean Waves* (Graham Ibbeson, 1993); the Captain Scott memorial sculpture (Jonathan Williams, 2003); *Merchant Seafarer's War Memorial* (Brian Fell, 1996); *Water Tower* (William Pye, 2002); and seen here, *People Like Us* (John Clinch, 1993).

Mermaid Quay

Mermaid Quay is at the heart of the redeveloped Cardiff Bay and is a boarding point for boat trips around the Bay, and for fast boats that head through Barrage Locks to the Bristol Channel. These days this is a leading destination for eating and drinking, especially if the sun is shining, with restaurants, bars and cafés to suit all tastes and pockets. You can enjoy your meal or drink looking towards the Bay's landmark buildings or watching yachts sail across the Bay to the Barrage and Penarth.

Roald Dahl Plass

This public open space is named after the famous author (1916–90) who was born in Cardiff of Norwegian parents. Originally the Oval Basin, entrance to the huge former west dock, the Plass now forms a dramatic approach to Cardiff Bay and a venue for open-air concerts, festivals and other cultural events.

Techniquest

Fire a rocket. Race an electric car. Test your reaction times. Launch a hot-air balloon. Techniquest is a must for families with enquiring children of all ages. It features innumerable hands-on science and technology puzzles and activities, plus a planetarium and a theatre where all sorts of dramatic and scientific things happen.

Mermaid Quay

What's on telly?

A new digital media centre is planned as part of the regeneration of former railway sidings in Porth Teigar at Cardiff Bay. The scheme also includes what is known as the 'BBC Wales Drama Village' situated nearby in the Roath Basin area. It is here that the BBC's longest running soap opera, *Pobol y Cwm*, is filmed, along with other TV favourites including *Casualty*, *Doctor Who* and *Upstairs Downstairs*.

Sport in the Bay

The International Sports Village in Cardiff Bay has much to offer, including: Cardiff International Pool, which has an Olympic-size pool and many other facilities; Cardiff International White Water, specializing in exciting water sports such as white-water rafting and kayaking; and an ice arena where Wales's professional ice-hockey team, Cardiff Devils, play their home games.

Across the Bay

Beyond the Bay Barrage lies the hilltop and seaside town of Penarth. Although you have to work to find them, the views from Penarth Head back to Cardiff and over the Bristol Channel are worth the effort. The seafront has a beach, a charming pier and an esplanade with, further on, fine clifftop walks to Lavernock Point. In Penarth town centre are two small but excellent galleries.

The pier

The marina

Penarth Esplanade

Penarth has a pleasant old-fashioned seafront with a beach, gardens and one of Britain's charming smaller piers, distinctive for its turquoise-roofed pavilion. Two hundred or so metres long, (658 feet, to be exact), the pier was built in 1894 to serve the paddle steamers plying the Bristol Channel. The *Waverley*, with its marine colleague the *Balmoral*, still calls here quite often in summer. In any case, the walk to the end on a clear day is rewarded by splendid views to the islands of Flat Holm and Steep Holm, and the Somerset coast beyond.

Penarth Marina

If you like watching other people mess about in boats, then there is no better place in the Bay than the entrance to Penarth's marina, near the Barrage locks. You can sit here and watch boats enter and leave the marina and also stroll across to see the barrage locks in operation. Nearby are some distinguished Victorian buildings, including the old Custom House, now two upmarket restaurants.

Cardiff Bay Barrage

The Barrage has been the catalyst for changing a mud-filled, little-used harbour into a freshwater lake and haven for pleasurecraft. In turn, this sparkling scene has given impetus to the rejuvenation of Cardiff's redundant docklands.

The Barrage, 1,200 yards (1.1km) long, consists of an embankment; three locks, with bascule bridges to allow traffic across; five sluices to regulate the flow of water in and out of the bay; and a fish pass, which allows migrating sea trout and salmon to return to the Rivers Taff and Ely to spawn. You can reach the Barrage either on foot, by waterbus or road train from Mermaid Quay.

Cardiff Bay Barrage

Two superb galleries

Close together in the town centre, Penarth has two galleries of different character but equal quality. ffotogallery on Plymouth Road, as its name suggests, focuses on photography and lens-based media of all types. Works are displayed in a unique, purpose-built Victorian building opposite the old railway station, now a pub. Just up the road are the smart, cool rooms of the Oriel Washington Gallery (aka Oriel Washington; 'oriel' means 'gallery' in Welsh). This was created from a former cinema as a charitable trust to showcase work by local professional artists and sculptors. The café down below is excellent too.

Washington Gallery

The views

There are two places to go for the best views. Paget Road (off Queens Road) looks across the marina and the bay area to the city centre. Penarth Head (off Clive Crescent), hidden in Victorian suburbia, offers views south over the pier and Esplanade and east across the Severn Estuary.

View towards Cardiff from Penarth

St Fagans National History Museum

Set in beautiful countryside four miles west of Cardiff's suburbs is one of Europe's finest open-air museums – and Wales's most visited heritage attraction. Opened in 1948 in the lovely wooded grounds of St Fagans Castle, it shows, through authentic reconstructions of real buildings, how the people of Wales lived, worked and played in the past.

The Castle

One of the finest Elizabethan manor houses in Wales, the castle, built in 1580, was extensively remodelled over succeeding centuries. It now reflects the lives of the Earl of Plymouth's family in the late 19th century, with glimpses of how it looked in previous eras. The castle is also notable for its superb 18-acre (7.2-hectare) gardens.

Celtic Village

To begin at the beginning, one of the most popular places at St Fagans, within a palisade in the woods, is a settlement of three circular Iron Age dwellings, recreated faithfully and based on actual remains found. All have straw roofs held up by varying types of wall. Inside are the everyday utensils that families of 3,000 years ago would have used. From time to time, experiments in crop rearing and livestock rearing take place here.

Something for everyone

In addition to the castle and its lovely gardens are galleries within the exhibition centre. These feature items of Welsh culture that merit special display, and the museum has an all-year-round calendar of events, staging traditional festivals and customs with music and dance.

The 100-acre (40-hectare) site also includes many other historic properties, including the charming Gwalia Stores. This emporium from Ogmore Vale, Bridgend, was originally built in 1880 and is shown today as it would have been in the late 1920s – and there is a tearoom upstairs.

Rhyd-y-Car Ironworkers' Houses, a terrace of cottages first built in Merthyr Tydfil in 1800, are a particular magnet for visitors. The six structurally identical dwellings and their gardens have been equipped to show how they might have looked during the intervening years from 1805 to 1985. A walk along the row is a fascinating trip through time.

Gwalia Stores

Llandaff

It's very easy to drive past this pretty 'village within a city', without realizing what a little gem of a place lies but a very few yards away. With its green, its cathedral in a hollow and the River Taff a short walk away through fields, Llandaff is definitely not to be missed.

Interior of Llandaff Cathedral

Llandaff Green

This charming, peaceful sward of grass, surrounded by houses of varying antiquity, could be a village green deep in the country, rather than a suburb of Cardiff. On the green itself is an imposing statue of James Rice Buckley (1878–1924), a former archdeacon of Llandaff. Towards the cathedral stands a fine memorial to those who died in the First World War. From here, the Dean's Steps make an attractive, if steep, approach to the cathedral's west door.

Llandaff Cathedral

The ancient Celtic cross near the cathedral's chapter house is almost the only remaining element of the monastery which St Teilo founded by the banks of the Taff in the 6th century AD. The saint's tomb is on the south side of the sanctuary (altar area), the metal frieze below it depicting scenes from the saint's life. The present building was begun *c.*1170, and includes many items of note, including: the Romanesque Urban Arch; Sir Jacob Epstein's striking figure of Majestas (Christ in Majesty); and examples of Pre-Raphaelite art, featuring famous names such as D.G. Rossetti, William Morris and Edward Burne-Jones.

Bishop's Palace

At the south-east end of Llandaff Green are the picturesque ruins of a gatehouse which was constructed in the 13th century. Given to the city and restored in the early 1970s, it leads to the grounds of the ancient palace where past Bishops of Llandaff resided.

Llandaff Cathedral

Beyond Cardiff

The Vale of Glamorgan is the broad promontory of land to the south and west of Cardiff, rolling its rural way through lanes and pretty stone villages down to the Heritage Coast. North of the city are superb mountains intersected by steep valleys and lovely vales. Guarding the entrance from one area to another, as it were, is the delightful Bute/Burges fantasy Castell Coch.

Castell Coch

With its conical towers rising from the trees, Castell Coch (meaning 'Red Castle' in Welsh), six miles north-west of Cardiff, resembles an illustration from a Victorian fairytale. This fantastical creation was, like Cardiff Castle, the brainchild of the 3rd Marquess of Bute and architect William Burges.

Built in the 1870s on the surviving foundations of the ruined 13th-century 'Red Castle', it overlooks the gorge of the River Taff. As with Cardiff, Bute gave Burges a free hand to explore their love of all things medieval. The result was a similar feast of decoration and symbolism. Again, no expense was spared and, like Burges's work at Cardiff, it is far better seen than described.

Castell Coch

Cowbridge

Cowbridge, 12 miles west of Cardiff, is a treat: a pretty and historic market town with a surprising variety of good-quality independent shops and eating places. Its wealth of ancient buildings includes the Town Hall on High Street, which houses a small museum. Cowbridge's many charming alleyways may take you to Holy Cross Church, the ancient grammar school and a physic garden first laid out in the 18th century. Within a few minutes' drive are Plas Llanmihangel, a 16th-century fortified manor house, Llanerch Vineyard and Dyffryn Gardens, one of the finest and largest landscaped gardens to be seen in Wales.

Glamorgan Heritage Coast

South-west of Cardiff, the pretty villages, lanes and farmland of the Vale of Glamorgan give way to a superb limestone coastline of cliffs and beaches, which offer opportunities for visitors of all tastes. For the energetic, the 18-mile (29-km) walk from Gileston in the east to Ogmore in the west affords lovely views of the coast and across the water to Somerset and Devon. For the aquatic-

Llancaiach Fawr Manor

To visit Llancaiach Fawr, 15 miles north of Cardiff, is to enjoy far more than just a fine manor house, built in 1530 and beautifully restored as it would have been in 1645. Here, history comes to life, and you are welcomed into the family home of Colonel Edward Prichard, Commissioner of Array to King Charles I. The master is temporarily absent on Civil War business and guests are shown around by the servants performing their daily duties. At all times the language and lives of the time are faithfully observed, making this unique experience one of Wales's top visitor attractions.

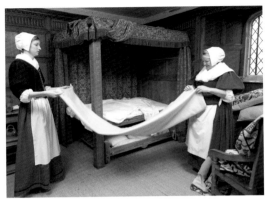

Llancaiach Fawr Manor

Caerphilly Castle

One of Britain's finest and largest fortresses, Caerphilly, with its massive towers and wide water defences, was largely completed in 1271 by Gilbert de Clare, Marcher Lord of Glamorgan, to protect his domains in Glamorgan from Prince Llywelyn ap Gruffudd. However, Llywelyn was defeated and killed by the English under Edward I, and the castle became better known for feasting than it was for fighting.

It fell into disrepair, but in 1776, became Bute family property. The 3rd Marquess re-roofed the Great Hall and had detailed plans made of the ruins. His son, the 4th Marquess, had much of the castle rebuilt in its original form. Today the castle, dominating the town, is a major visitor venue in the care of Cadw, and its peaceful surroundings offer a place to sit by the water, do some fishing or feed the many birds that live here.

Caerphilly Castle

minded, several sandy beaches offer bathing and surfing, while there are many lovely spots to sit and read a book, or just take in the scenery.

The Heritage Coast Visitor Centre is located at Dunraven Bay, near Southerndown, one of the most popular and scenic beaches. Nearby are the extensive dunes by the estuary of the River Ogmore, the walk from the car park through the sand hills being rewarded with a golden beach and wonderful views.

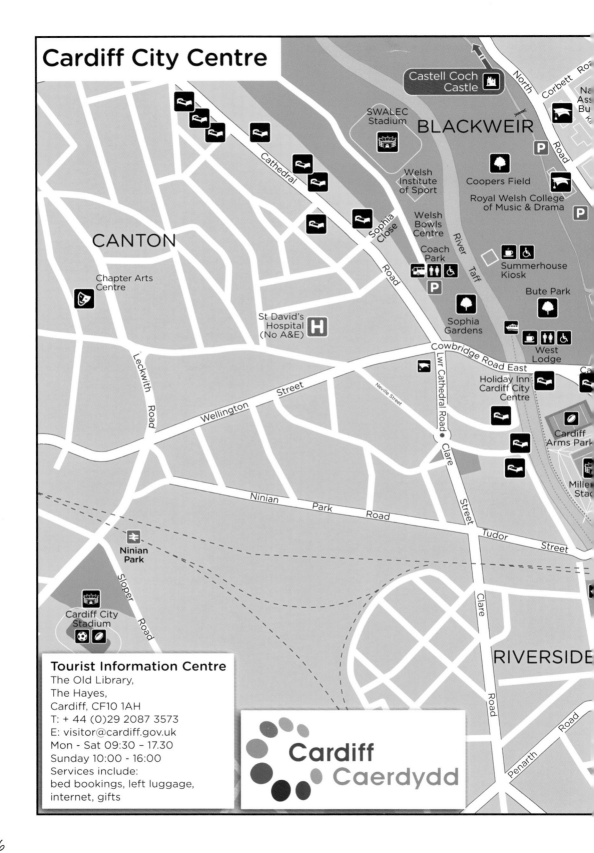

Cardiff City Centre

Castell Coch Castle

SWALEC Stadium

BLACKWEIR

Coopers Field

Welsh Institute of Sport

Royal Welsh College of Music & Drama

Welsh Bowls Centre

Summerhouse Kiosk

Coach Park

Bute Park

CANTON

Sophia Close

River Taff

Chapter Arts Centre

Sophia Gardens

West Lodge

St David's Hospital (No A&E)

Cowbridge Road East

Holiday Inn Cardiff City Centre

Cardiff Arms Park

Lwr Cathedral Road

Neville Street

Wellington Street

Street

Leckwith Road

Clare Street

Millennium Stadium

Ninian Park Road

Tudor Street

Ninian Park

Clare Road

Sloper Road

RIVERSIDE

Cardiff City Stadium

Penarth Road

Tourist Information Centre
The Old Library,
The Hayes,
Cardiff, CF10 1AH
T: + 44 (0)29 2087 3573
E: visitor@cardiff.gov.uk
Mon - Sat 09:30 – 17.30
Sunday 10:00 - 16:00
Services include:
bed bookings, left luggage,
internet, gifts

Cardiff
Caerdydd

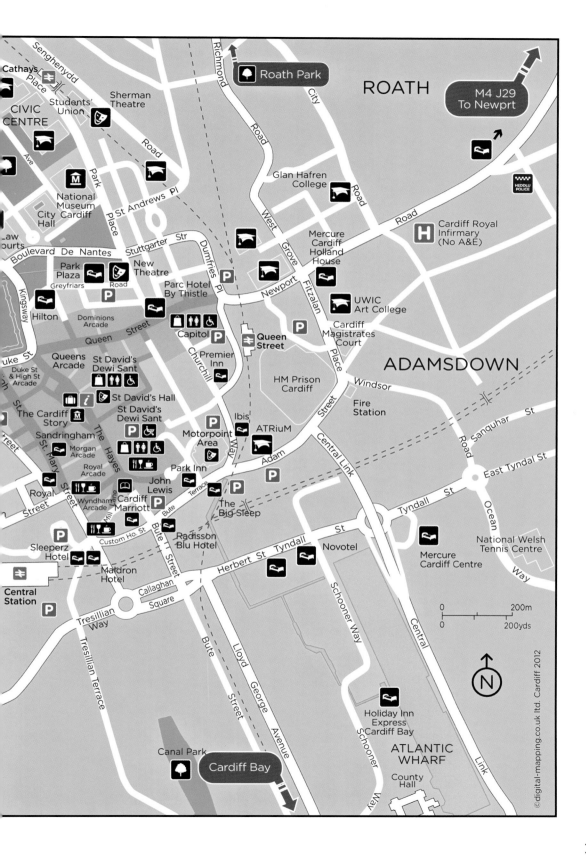

Roath Park

ROATH

M4 J29
To Newprt

Cathays
Place

Sherman
Theatre

CIVIC
CENTRE

Students'
Union

Glan Hafren
College

Cardiff Royal
Infirmary
(No A&E)

HEDDLU
POLICE

Road

Park

National
Museum

City Cardiff
Hall

St Andrews Pl

Place

Mercure
Cardiff
Holland
House

Road

Law
Courts

Boulevard De Nantes

Stuttgarter Str

New
Theatre

UWIC
Art College

Park
Plaza

Greyfriars

Road

Parc Hotel
By Thistle

Newport

Cardiff
Magistrates
Court

ADAMSDOWN

Kingsway

Hilton

Dominions
Arcade

Queen Street

Capitol

Queen
Street

Churchill

Premier
Inn

HM Prison
Cardiff

Windsor

Fire
Station

Sanquhar St

Queens
Arcade

St David's
Dewi Sant

Duke St
& High St
Arcade

St David's Hall

The Cardiff
Story

St David's
Dewi Sant

Ibis

ATRiUM

Adam

Central Link

East Tyndal St

Sandringham

Morgan
Arcade

Motorpoint
Area

Street

Tyndall St

Ocean

Royal
Arcade

Park Inn

Way

National Welsh
Tennis Centre

Royal
Street

Wyndham
Arcade

Cardiff
Marriott

John
Lewis

Terrace

Bute

The
Big Sleep

St

Tyndall

Novotel

Mercure
Cardiff Centre

Way

Sleeperz
Hotel

Custom Ho. St

Bute T Street

Radisson
Blu Hotel

Herbert St

Central
Station

Maldron
Hotel

Callaghan
Square

Tresillian
Way

Tresillian Terrace

Bute

Street

Lloyd George

Avenue

Schooner Way

Central

Link

Canal Park

Cardiff Bay

Schooner

Holiday Inn
Express
Cardiff Bay

Way

ATLANTIC
WHARF

County
Hall

0   200m
0   200yds

N

©digital-mapping.co.uk ltd. Cardiff 2012

27

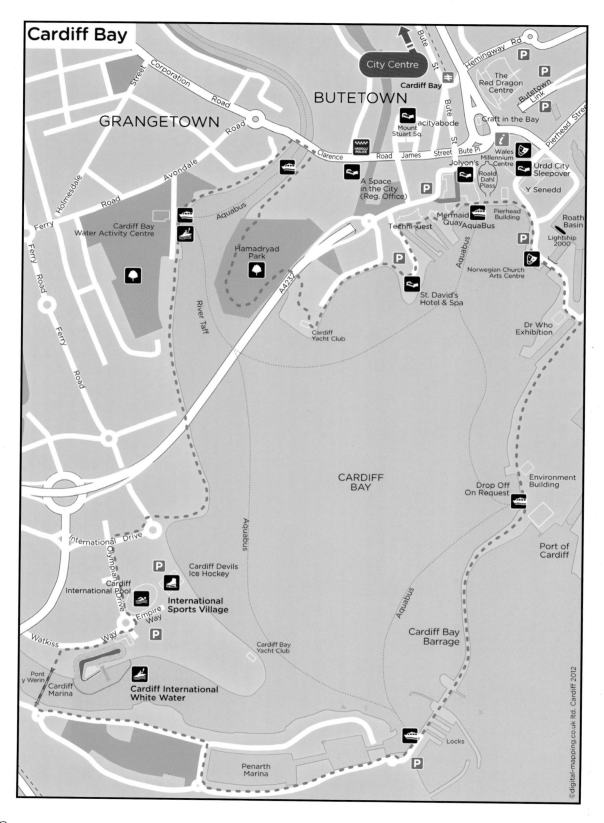

Cardiff Bay

GRANGETOWN

BUTETOWN

City Centre

Cardiff Bay

The Red Dragon Centre

Butetown Link

Craft in the Bay

Mount Stuart Sq.

acityabode

HEDDLU POLICE

Clarence Road

James Street

Bute Pl

Wales Millennium Centre

Jolyon's

Roald Dahl Plass

Urdd City Sleepover

Y Senedd

A Space in the City (Reg. Office)

Cardiff Bay Water Activity Centre

Mermaid Quay

Pierhead Building

AquaBus

Roath Basin

Lightship 2000

Techniquest

Hamadryad Park

Norwegian Church Arts Centre

St. David's Hotel & Spa

Cardiff Yacht Club

Dr Who Exhibition

River Taff

Aquabus

CARDIFF BAY

Environment Building

Drop Off On Request

Port of Cardiff

International Drive

Cardiff International Pool

Cardiff Devils Ice Hockey

International Sports Village

Cardiff Bay Yacht Club

Aquabus

Cardiff Bay Barrage

Empire Way

Watkiss Way

Pont y Werin

Cardiff Marina

Cardiff International White Water

Locks

Penarth Marina

Olympian Drive

©digital-mapping.co.uk ltd. Cardiff 2012